Siberian Huskies

Lyn Sirota

MEDIA ENHANCED BOOKS
AV2 BY WEIGL™
ADDED VALUE · AUDIO VISUAL

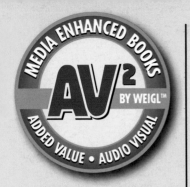

AV² provides enriched content that supplements and complements this book. Weigl's AV² books strive to create inspired learning and engage young minds in a total learning experience.

Your AV² Media Enhanced books come alive with...

Audio
Listen to sections of the book read aloud.

Key Words
Study vocabulary, and complete a matching word activity.

Go to **www.av2books.com,** and enter this book's unique code.

BOOK CODE

LBQ28589

Video
Watch informative video clips.

Quizzes
Test your knowledge.

Embedded Weblinks
Gain additional information for research.

Slide Show
View images and captions, and prepare a presentation.

AV² by Weigl brings you media enhanced books that support active learning.

Try This!
Complete activities and hands-on experiments.

... and much, much more!

Published by AV² by Weigl
350 5th Avenue, 59th Floor
New York, NY 10118
Website: www.av2books.com

Library of Congress Control Number: 2017960032

ISBN 978-1-4896-7368-8 (hardcover)
ISBN 978-1-4896-7960-4 (softcover)
ISBN 978-1-4896-7369-5 (multi-user eBook)

Printed in the United States of America in Brainerd, Minnesota
1 2 3 4 5 6 7 8 9 0   22 21 20 19 18

012018
120817

Project Coordinator: John Willis   Art Director: Terry Paulhus

Every reasonable effort has been made to trace ownership and to obtain permission to reprint copyright material. The publisher would be pleased to have any errors or omissions brought to its attention so that they may be corrected in subsequent printings.

Weigl acknowledges Getty Images and Alamy as its primary image suppliers for this title.

Siberian Huskies

Contents

Name That Dog

What friendly dog loves to run?

What medium-sized dog comes from northeast Asia?

What high-energy dog is the 12th most popular breed?

What dog is known for pulling a sled and racing in the Iditarod?

Did you say the Siberian husky?

Then you are right !

Sled Dog

The Siberian husky was originally bred by the native Chukchi people of northeastern Asia thousands of years ago. They lived in an area of Siberia that was close to Alaska. The Chukchi needed a strong dog breed that could travel long distances in the snow. When their climate became colder, they required a dog that could carry people and things by sled. This is when the term "sled dog" began.

The people of Siberia could travel much greater distances with a sled dog than they could by walking. These dogs were used as pack animals, carrying food and other supplies. They traveled with the Chukchi people to the sea to haul food. They also traveled with them to hunt.

Siberia is separated from Alaska by the Bering Sea. Today, it belongs to Russia.

Arctic Ocean

East Siberian Sea

Chukchi Sea

Beauford Sea

Russia

Bering Strait

Alaska (United States)

Bering Sea

Gulf of Alaska

Siberian huskies are admired for their skills as sled dogs. In 1925, there was a serious illness called **diphtheria** that broke out in Nome, Alaska. The people there needed special medicine. The only way to transport the medicine was by using sled dogs. Siberian huskies traveled more than 600 miles (966 kilometers) in five and a half days to save the people of Nome. The sled dog that finally delivered the medicine was named Balto. There is a well-known statue of Balto in New York City's Central Park.

Chukchi dogs were first introduced to Alaska in 1908 to compete in the long-distance All Alaska Sweepstakes race.

Sled dogs are used to the cold. They can work and play in temperatures as low as −75 degrees Fahrenheit (−59 degrees Celsius).

Arctic Coat

Siberian huskies have a thicker coat of fur than most other dog breeds. They have a double coat that is made up of a soft undercoat and a longer, stiffer top coat. Huskies are medium-sized, quick, and graceful. They can carry a light load at medium speed for long distances. Their muscles are firm and developed. Like ballet dancers, they appear light on their feet.

Huskies have a bushy tail that they carry curled over their backs. Their tails help to protect their faces from snow and wind when they curl up on the ground. Their large "snowshoe" paws have hair between the toes to help keep their feet warm. This hair also helps them grip ice for balance. These traits make Siberian huskies well-equipped for snowy, cold temperatures. They are not built for warm, humid climates. When they are in a warm environment, they need plenty of water and shade.

Huskies clean themselves regularly and have very little smell. However, their double coat needs consistent brushing.

A handsome breed, huskies have a wolf-like appearance. Their heads may have a black-and-white or red-and-white pattern. Their coats may be solid black or white. They can be a mixture of black, white, red, brown, silver, or gray. Their triangle-shaped ears open forward, and their almond-shaped eyes make them look alert and ready for action. Husky eyes can be blue, brown, amber, or a combination of colors. They may have one blue and one brown eye. Their distinct look makes them popular in books and films.

The American Kennel Club (AKC) recognizes 18 different color combinations and 4 different types of marking for huskies.

Smart Breed

While huskies are known to be extremely **independent**, they are also quite social. Their loving nature makes them good family pets. However, being so social does have a downside. Huskies do not make good watchdogs. They will welcome anyone with a wagging tail! They are also not a barking breed. They will not alert a family to visitors. Huskies communicate with howling sounds, like wolves. This howl can be heard up to 10 miles (16 km) away.

Huskies are intelligent, learn quickly, and may be stubborn. Training them can be tricky because they get bored easily. Playing, running, and digging are some of their favorite activities. Giving them toys, space to play, and plenty of exercise is important for their development.

High-energy, intelligent dogs, such as huskies, enjoy games of fetch and tug-of-war.

It is a good idea to use a leash when running with a husky. Some like to run off or chase small animals.

Huskies can run at speeds of 28 miles (45 km) per hour.

Huskies make great exercise partners while running or biking, especially when the weather is cooler. They need a high level of activity or else they can become **destructive**. Huskies, like other dog breeds, should not be left alone for long periods of time. These smart canines are known escape artists. Securing and containing them with proper fencing or a kennel is extremely important. They also need to be watched while outside.

Husky Puppies

Healthy Siberian husky females have between four and six puppies in a litter. Purebred Siberian husky puppies come from breeders. Finding the right breeder helps avoid health issues. Not all breeders have the same standards and **ethics**. For these reasons, doing research and asking questions is important when deciding where to find a Siberian husky puppy.

Huskies typically have black, brown, or red noses. Some are born with a "snow nose." A snow nose will turn light pink in the winter and darken again in spring.

Husky puppies do not open their eyes until they are two to four weeks old.

Selecting the right puppy from a litter takes time. Visiting with puppies to see how they act with people will help. Looking at their eyes, coat, skin, and teeth is also a good way to see how breeders care for their dogs. At about 8 to 10 weeks, husky puppies can leave their mothers.

The best time to plan and organize is before bringing a puppy home. Selecting a good veterinarian and dog food to get started with are important when preparing for a puppy. Husky pups love to be busy and have fun! They need a safe environment to sleep and play in, with a variety of toys. Chew toys help calm teething pain and pressure when their new teeth come in.

It is a good idea to change out a husky's toys once a week. This helps to keep the dog's interest and keeps toys from wearing out.

During long-distance races, such as the Iditarod, teams of up to 16 dogs will pull a sled for 12 or more hours a day.

Huskies at Work

The Siberian husky is a relative of the ancient Siberian wolf. **Genetic testing** and other research has shown that this **prehistoric** wolf lives on in Arctic sled dogs. At one time, scientists thought that huskies came from gray wolves. Scientists now know gray wolves and huskies share **ancestors**.

Huskies love people, children, and other dogs. They are instinctively pack-oriented. This means they like being part of a group. Their behavior in a pack is different. Their senses are **keen** and they are on high alert. **Mushers** train huskies to pull sleds. Pulling a sled is a team effort, so these animals work together to run, pull, and haul. Huskies have an impressive record at the Iditarod Trail International Sled Dog Race. It is the world's longest sled-dog event, spanning across Alaska for 1,049 miles (1,688 km).

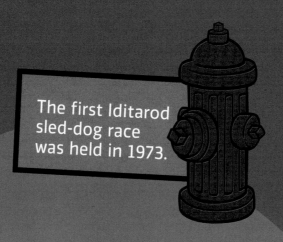

The first Iditarod sled-dog race was held in 1973.

Pulling a sled is not the only sport for huskies. With proper training, they can participate in weight pulling and carting. Both of these activities involve pulling and running. Huskies can also be trained for skatejoring. Skatejoring is when a dog pulls a person while they are skating or skateboarding.

Because a busy husky is a happy dog, it can also be trained for **agility**. This involves off-leash running through a course. A more low-key activity is therapy work. A dog visiting people in hospitals and nursing homes can brighten up a patient's day. It is perfect for such a social dog and can help patients feel happy and more connected with the world.

Huskies can be trained in dog carting for fun, competition, and exercise.

Huskies are social animals. They need a lot of play and interaction with other dogs or their owners.

Caring for a Siberian Husky

Huskies are considered a healthy dog breed. Some areas of concern are their hips and their eyes. At times, they may have minor skin, **respiratory**, or **digestive** conditions. These can be treated by a veterinarian.

Because huskies are an active, working breed, they need to be exercised 30 to 60 minutes per day. Inactive dogs can become overweight and unhappy. The extra weight puts a strain on their bodies. Hip problems are common in huskies. Sometimes, their hips can become weak or painful.

The typical life span of a husky is 12 to 15 years.

Mainly due to their looks, Siberian huskies are one of the most wrongly purchased dog breeds. People forget to research their **quirky** personalities before they bring the dogs home. Then, the owners are surprised by some of the huskies' behaviors. Some of these behaviors are their need to dig and run.

Regular veterinary appointments and vaccinations are part of being a responsible pet owner. Owners can help keep huskies healthy, too. By watching their huskies, owners will know how they normally act. If a dog begins to act differently, it may have a health issue. Understanding their pets helps owners enjoy these companions for a long time.

Young huskies should visit the vet once a month for vaccinations and wellness checks.

Siberian Husky Quiz

Q: Where do Siberian huskies come from?

A: Northeastern Asia

Q: How many puppies do huskies usually have in a litter?

A: Between four and six

Q: What is the name of the famous sled dog who helped save the people of Nome, Alaska?

A: Balto

Q: The Siberian husky is a relative of what wild animal?

A: The Siberian wolf

Q: What do other dogs do that huskies do not?

A: Bark

Q: How long do huskies usually live?

A: 12 to 15 years

Key Words

agility (uh-JILL-lih-tee): the ability to move quickly and easily

ancestors (ANN-sess-turs): people or animals in the same family who lived in the past

destructive (dee-STRUHK-tiv): causing great harm or damage

digestive (dye-JES-tiv): relating to the process of digesting food

diphtheria (dip-THEE-re-uh): a disease that can infect the body in the tonsils, nose, throat, or skin

ethics (ETH-iks): the main ideas of right and wrong

genetic testing (juh-NET-ik TESS-ting): studying DNA to find links between living things

independent (in-deh-PEN-dent): free from outside control

keen (KEEN): sharp or penetrating

mushers (MUHSH-urs): the drivers of a dogsled

prehistoric (pree-hi-STOR-ik): a period of time before written records; ancient

quirky (KWURK-ee): characterized by peculiar, unexpected traits

respiratory (RES-pur-uh-tor-ee): relating to breathing

Index

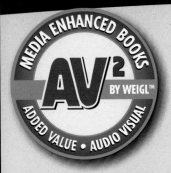

Log on to www.av2books.com

AV² by Weigl brings you media enhanced books that support active learning. Go to www.av2books.com, and enter the special code found on page 2 of this book. You will gain access to enriched and enhanced content that supplements and complements this book. Content includes video, audio, weblinks, quizzes, a slide show, and activities.

AV² Online Navigation

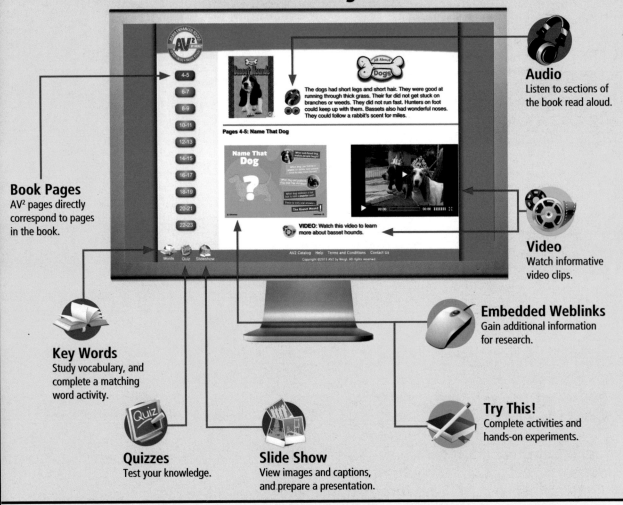

Book Pages
AV² pages directly correspond to pages in the book.

Audio
Listen to sections of the book read aloud.

Video
Watch informative video clips.

Key Words
Study vocabulary, and complete a matching word activity.

Embedded Weblinks
Gain additional information for research.

Quizzes
Test your knowledge.

Slide Show
View images and captions, and prepare a presentation.

Try This!
Complete activities and hands-on experiments.

AV² was built to bridge the gap between print and digital. We encourage you to tell us what you like and what you want to see in the future.

Sign up to be an AV² Ambassador at www.av2books.com/ambassador.

Due to the dynamic nature of the Internet, some of the URLs and activities provided as part of AV² by Weigl may have changed or ceased to exist. AV² by Weigl accepts no responsibility for any such changes. All media enhanced books are regularly monitored to update addresses and sites in a timely manner. Contact AV² by Weigl at 1-866-649-3445 or av2books@weigl.com with any questions, comments, or feedback.